I0412544

The Goal Achiever

The Ultimate 9 Steps to achieve a Full Scholarship

Jen Vuhuong

Today, let's make a decision to step up in life!

'Ask what MEANING do you want to give to a

scholarship instead of what the scholarship will give you.

When you do it, not only the scholarship but other

opportunity will welcome you. You are not only a

TAKER but a GIVER and a goal achiever.'

- Jen, your friend, personal development coach and

trainer

Jenvuhuong.com/thegoalachiever

Copyright ©2018 by Jen Vuhuong

(4th edition: 2018)

I dedicate this book to my younger sister Quynh, my eldest sister Lan, my second-eldest sister Toi, my elder brother Tien, and to my parents for bringing me into this world. I would like to say, 'Thank you' for inspiring me to be 'Non-stop living, loving and giving' every moment of my life!

I love you all.

Message to my Future Scholars, Future Leaders

Have you ever felt that you could explode because you had been keeping something to yourself for so long but you had not shared it with others in a way that could be beneficial to their lives yet? I have been struggling with this feeling myself after over 7 years of applying for various scholarships. I cannot express how grateful am for the 5 scholarships which were awarded to me, particularly Erasmus and Chevening, which allowed me to study a full master's degree in Spain and another one in the UK. These were two of the most important milestones in my life. Therefore, I feel compelled to share what I have learned with others, who are now walking on the same journey – developing ourselves and thriving to achieve a goal to make a contribution to life.

I truly believe that if we can share what we have been through with other people, we will feel more fulfilled because someone else will benefit from it. At the same time, it will be a way of expressing our gratitude for the opportunities that we have had. It is even better if this can inspire the readers to share their experience with others after their own achievement.

If you are reading this book, it is for you. You will find it is about more than achieving a scholarship, rather it is about accomplishing anything in your life; as long as you are ready, you trust in yourself, and you take action on it. I am honoured because our journeys in pursuing our life goals have crossed here. I am looking forward to seeing you step up in life. You deserve it and you can do it!

Let us Non-stop love, live, give to achieve great things every moment of life!

What will you find in this book?

'The PART of yourself that helps you to achieve a goal such as a full scholarship'.

This book aims to convey the message that deep within each of us lies an undying passion and potential for stepping UP in life and CONTRIBUTING to life that can help us overcome any challenges so we can achieve our true desire. To win a full scholarship is an exhibition of that desire which can be achieved through continuous action based on the right mindset and the right strategy. The book includes a map with 9 ultimate steps that can be used to take action everyday to make things happen, not only achieving a scholarship but also achieving other individual goals that you might have.

While you are reading this book or after you have read it, is to put any idea into action at the very moment it clicks in your brain. **Read it over and over again (at least 3 times) to convert KNOWLEDGE to ACTION and**

action to RESULTS. Don't let the doubt settle in. Don't let struggles stop you. Don't let your passion of achieving a scholarship fall asleep! Let's do it TODAY!

Let's join the journey together!

Contents

Introduction to My journey as a Scholar

'It is impossible. Be realistic! Remember, you are just a little girl from the countryside. Just stay at home, get married and have a bus load of kids'. That was what a friend of my father's told me after hearing about my desire to go abroad to open my mind and to help more people. He was one of many acquaintances who directed my thoughts on the 'impossibility' of going abroad.

I was one of the most stubborn kids in my village, so I didn't believe what others told me only until I experienced it. There was no evidence that I couldn't do it. Most importantly, I had to make it happen to help my family and the people around me to have a better life. I didn't want to see them struggle with life, even when they were working hard everyday.

My parents worked at four different jobs to bring up myself and my siblings. I was saved by my family from being kidnapped, from a serious motorbike accident in which I lost almost 1 litre of blood, and from an incident of almost drowning in a river. I told myself that I had to realise my desire, not only for myself, but also for those who had worked so hard to make sure that I had the best life they could give me.

I studied hard, disciplined myself with the desire of going abroad one day. I woke up early everyday, studied everywhere when riding a buffalo or cooking or going to the toilet (this is an interesting habit do you think so? But it was truly effective for me to read in the toilet because I felt nobody distracted me). I entered the top science and technology university in Vietnam ('Bach Khoa') where I could find good opportunities to obtain a scholarship to study in Western countries. I also disciplined myself to study seven days a week in the library with the desire of one day achieving a scholarship to study abroad.

When I was a second-year student, I shared with a respectful senior student my desire of obtaining a full scholarship in order to go abroad. He told me I could not do this. I blindly believed in what he said (or maybe I myself had doubts regarding my own desire that I did not consciously know; or the determined part of me was scared of a new challenge). I believed that I couldn't go abroad anymore. I felt lost. I felt disappointed. I felt my effort for more than ten years wasn't going to pay off. I found my ambition trapped in my home country. However, deep down within me, I knew that I would find a way. I knew that I could at least keep trying my best in studying.

I applied to become a researcher in one of my faculty's labs – Electronics and Telecommunications. I had an opportunity to work with a team of three boys and with two supervisors whom I considered the best in my faculty. Everyone in my team planned to go abroad as an obvious thing to do and that triggered my deep desire. One day, I shared my desire with one of my supervisors. She immediately told me 'Why not? You can do it.' I trusted and admired her so I believed I could go abroad for studying. I believed again in my desire of going abroad to raise my standards in Western education then helps my own country Vietnam.

Doubts disappeared, strong belief and nonstop action stayed. From 2009 to 2015 I won 5 different scholarships, including 2 world's top scholarships – Erasmus and Chevening – to study in Spain and the UK. I couldn't express how very thankful I felt to have these opportunities. It has been a life-changing experience for me. I could experience good education systems, travel around to immerse myself in different cultures, learn and work with international friends to bring my business to another level. Most importantly, I realised the successful patterns of achieving a desire, a goal and a dream, to turn the IMPOSSIBLE into the 'I'M POSSIBLE'. I would like to share the patterns and the experiences with you. I believe in you and your dream of raising your standards to make a difference in your life and the world.

Let's make it happen!

Love with respect,

Jen,

The following ideas have accumulated from my experience of achieving 5 scholarships and that of achieving other goals such as changing my career from engineering to training, lessons learned from successful people, and my interviews with over 100 people who have achieved certain successes, including over 50 SMEs' business owners and over 50 scholars from all over the world (updated data upto 2018). Just take action, model these strategies to utilise your own opportunities and resources to achieve a scholarship or a personal goal

based on your best true self.

The motivation of the book

- **For future scholars and leaders:** You are the inspiration for me and for many other scholars to come out and share our experiences.

- **My life's mission is to empower future leaders by sharing my experience:**

  - My experience of seven years of applying for different scholarships and achieving five different scholarships (including Erasmus and British government scholarship Chevening to study master's in Spain and the UK).

  - Being fortunate enough to have interviewed more than 50 scholars from all over the world.

  - Experience of studying, working and living in more than 15 countries around the globe.

  - Being fortunate to be saved from death more than three times and to realise that the secret of success is to give joyfully. This book is my gratitude for life.

How to make the best of the book

- Keep an open mind: the mission of this book is to provide you a big picture – a system of mindset and good habits collecting from people who achieved scholarships or successful people so you can apply the system to maximize your true potential to achieve any goal especially a full scholarship. Hence, you will not see a lot of personal examples of applications or motivation letters from me or other scholars (these I believe you could easily find in the internet) rather you will see a systematic way of thinking, crucial evaluating factors and action you need to take to be your best.

- Stay until the last page.

- Trust in your journey and most importantly trust in yourself that 'you can do it'.

- Read over and over again, at least 3 times to turn ideas into actions and actions into results.

- The 9 ideas work best when they are together, so you should read all 9 ideas to see the big picture and then return to each idea to re-evaluate the details.

- **Act now** - The right time for you to work on achieving a scholarship or any goal is TODAY – the day you have the desire to achieve it.

- Take immediate action at the very moment when an idea clicks within your brain.

- Give your best to each practice section, the scholarship, and life.

- Apply the 9 ideas for other personal goals in life.

- Share with people in the same journey as you. If you could find the way to make the ultimate 9 ideas in this book work the best for you or you could find other ideas to support for the effectiveness of these ideas, please do share it with others. You also can share it with our community and we will help you to spread your messages (you can send email to jenvuhuong@gmail.com).

The psychological and social foundation of this book?

'Eighty percent of success is due to psychology—

mindset, beliefs, and emotions—and only 20

percent is due to strategy.'

- Tony Robbins (

This book is built upon three central messages supported by practical steps **for** those who are looking to achieve a personal goal such as a full scholarship, most importantly stepping up to pursue their life's goals:

- **Mind** (80 percent of success): Position your mind to be like the minds of successful people and act bigger to get 'bigger' scholarships to better yourself to contribute more to society. The book guides you to develop a GROWTH and SERVICE mindset.

- **Strategies** (20 percent of success): Implementing strategies of people who have already achieved what you desire will give you a greater chance of success.

The book guides you to learn from successful people to be selective, strategic and to be your BEST TRUE SELF, which is your unique competitive advantage.

- **Daily strategic action (successful habits):** Daily action helps you to gain momentum to never to give up on your goal. The book guides you to strategically take ACTION every day and honour struggles to move towards your goal

YOUR MIND

You need to approach a scholarship from an inside-out approach (you take action to develop yourself everyday, you have values that make you deserve achieve a scholarship – developing intrinsic motivation) and not from an outside-out approach (you chase the scholarship because of the trend – depending on extrinsic motivation). When it is done inside, it will be done outside.

Big Idea 1: The why, the growth service mindset, the driver of any success

"You were put on this earth to achieve your greatest self, to live out your purpose, and to do it courageously."

— *Steve Maraboli*

When you apply for any scholarship, you need to answer the first and foremost question 'Why do you want to obtain a scholarship?' Your reasons for applying for a scholarship should be aligned with your life purpose, your life vision. Even if you don't have a clear purpose, you may want to focus on two fundamental factors to answer this question: growth mindset (e.g. to raise your standard) and service mindset (e.g. to contribute to society). Scholarship sponsors look for people who not only have a desire to better themselves by studying abroad but also who desire to make a contribution to society in their own countries or to the world. It is important to notice that the sponsors look for a return investment from you which is measured by your growth and your contribution to society. You are not only a TAKER but also a GIVER. You not only take the scholarship but also give your values to the scholarship by contributing later to your country and the people around you.

The principle of giving and receiving is also clearly exhibited in some of the other questions of scholarships. Take Chevening scholarship as an example, there are questions such as 'What will you contribute to the Chevening alumni network after coming back?' or 'What will you contribute to the relationship between Vietnam and the UK?'. Although you may think you have not experienced the time of studying abroad yet so you may not have a clear idea of what you can do, you need to ask yourself, 'What would be contribution after having such a great experience?'. You can refer to the benefits that you can gain from studying abroad then associate that values with the visionary and mission of your alumni network or your country or the diplomatic relations of your home country and the host country. I believe if you have the motivation to apply for a scholarship, you already have the seeds of 'GIVING BACK' in you, just take the time and critically ask yourself more often to find the right answer for you.

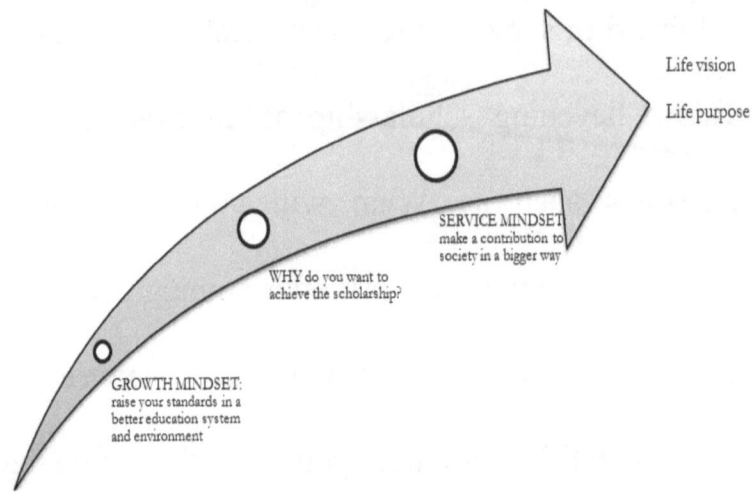

Maybe you already have a growth mindset and that is why you are applying for a scholarship so just continue developing this growth mindset. You should also appreciate the contribution that you made, are making and will make to life that reflects a growth mindset. To cultivate a growth and service mindset, you need to tune in to your intrinsic motivation rather than your extrinsic motivation.

An example of extrinsic motivation is to earn a famous award at a top university, while the intrinsic motivation is to challenge your best self to raise standards by studying within a high-quality educational environment so that later, you can help people in a greater way. Intrinsic motivation acts as an inner fire to keep you motivated regardless of your present situation, while extrinsic motivation is a short- term illusion because it comes from the outside and you cannot control external factors. Therefore, no matter what your first motivation is, the ultimate motivation should be intrinsic - '*You want to win a scholarship to raise your standards to help people in a bigger and better way.*'

Having a growth mindset also means that you never give up because you will always look at any event with an attitude of learning. If you don't get accepted when applying for a scholarship, you will learn from the experience to better yourself in your next application.

With a growth mindset, you will always move on. I failed twice in my application for an Erasmus scholarship before I achieved it. At least four among many scholars whom I interviewed told me that their first application for the scholarship failed, but they did not give up. A growth mindset also motivates you to learn from other successful people instead of feeling jealous or demotivated by thinking 'It is working for them, but not for me because I am not ready or I am not good enough.' The growth mindset will tell you 'If it is working for them, let me try. I am good and I can better myself everyday.'

The service mindset helps you to be aware of your values and what you can contribute to society. The service mindset will tell you that you can make a contribution to life no matter where you are at. You always have something to offer to life. The things you can offer can be simply an act of kindness such as saying hi to a security guard. It can also be you help others such as showing the road to a foreigner. It be can simply sharing what you have learned with others who are in the same development journey with you.

The service mindset also helps you and me to appreciate our own values. My sister is the person who has helped me deeply appreciate the service mindset in the best way because she always gives even in the most difficult situation of her life – dropping out of school, leg broken by accident. She always gives her kindness and care for others. My service mindset has been nurtured by my sister's service mindset from the little things such as a smile in the morning with a stranger to the self-belief and the dedication and desire of making a contribution to life.

The desire to go abroad to study and raise my standards to help more people on an international level has guided me, guarded me and assured my success in achieving different scholarships and other goals, such as getting the jobs that I loved. I never forget the burning desire shared in my application that I wanted to inspire young people to have a positive mindset and dedicate themselves to being the best human being and I wish myself to be the person to experience and do it then share with them. I also remember having an interviewer told me after the interview told me that she was convinced by the spirit and determination of my desire on developing myself and making a contribution to society. Scholars whom I interviewed also emphasised the importance of having a growth and service mindset – developing themselves, making a difference in their countries, and the relationships between their countries and the scholarship sponsors. Therefore, having a growth and service mindset and a desire to make a contribution to life will guide, guard, and assure your success too.

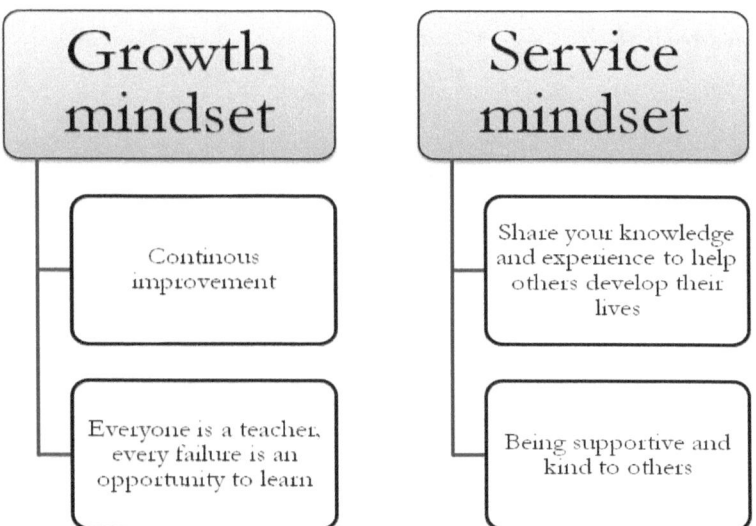

Call for action:

1. Write down your motivations in applying for a scholarship

3 reasons make me apply for a scholarship are:

...

...

...

2. Change from extrinsic motivations to intrinsic motivations

3 intrinsic motivation makes me want to achieve a scholarship:

...

...

...

(Intrinsic motivations should have two elements - growth (your desire to grow as a better person) and service (your desire to contribute to your countries and the people around you).

3. Cultivate the growth and service mindset.

To cultivate your Growth mindset:

- *Think about your past experiences (both failures and successes), write down what you can learn from these experiences to better your life. Keep in mind a question to ask yourself, no matter what happens in your life 'What can I learn from this experience?' and keep developing yourself and try again until you succeed.*

My one failure...

...

My one achievement is...

...

3 lessons I have leanred from the above experience are

...

...

...

- *Think about the people you have known, write down what you can learn from them. In any situation, no matter what people tell you, ask yourself 'What can I learn from that?'.*

  3 people I have learned the best are...

  3 lessons I have learned from these people are

  ...

  ...

  ...

To cultivate your Service mindset:

- *Write down something that you have been through which you consider to have been an important learning experience, and which may benefit people who are on the same journey as you. Challenge yourself to go to a local community or organisation to share your experience.*

3 things I have learned that I want to share with others

   ...

   ...

   ...

3 people/communities that I will share the above lessons are

   ...

   ...

   ...

- *Everyday, ask yourself 'How can I be nice to people around me? How can I support people around me?'*

3 kindness actions that I can take today are

…

…

…

Recommended books:

1. Mindset: The New Psychology of Success _ Carol S. Dweck

2. Rewire Your Brain: Think Your Way to a Better Life _ John B. Arden

Big Idea 2: The big thinking, the amplifier of any success

> 'The man who thinks he can and the man who thinks he
> can't are both usually right.
>
> Which one are you?'
>
> — Henry Ford

Now that you know why you want to achieve a scholarship, you know the driver of success in applying for a scholarship. Now, you want to achieve the best scholarship that you can. Thinking big helps you to amplify your action towards bigger results. How you position your thoughts at the beginning of your journey will direct your subsequent steps and actions. Bigger thinking will lead to bigger action, then bigger results will follow. When you think you can, all your subsequent actions will align with your capabilities, no matter where you start. When you think you cannot, all your subsequent actions will align with matters of which you not capable, no matter where or how close the goal is. Therefore, if you want to achieve a scholarship, you need to believe that you can achieve a scholarship. Furthermore, you should think bigger to get even 'bigger' scholarships (e.g. full scholarship rather than 50 percent scholarship; a full scholarship with higher fund rather than lower fund).

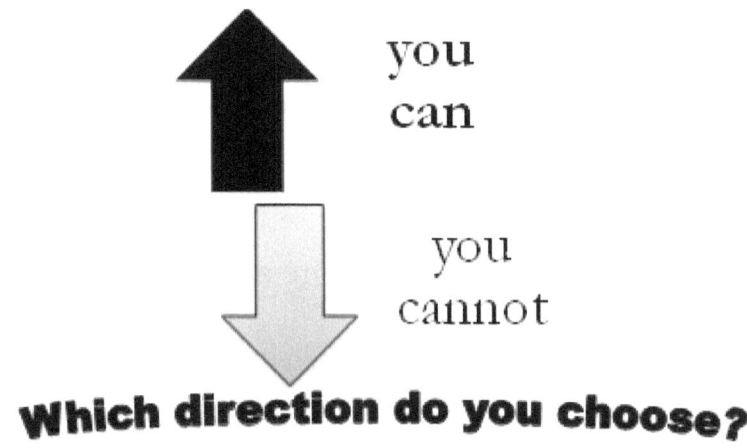

Which direction do you choose?

Let's take my case as an example. The first times that I applied for Erasmus scholarships from 2009 to 2011, I didn't believe that I would get it because I told myself that I didn't have much working experience. Therefore, I didn't make an effort to prepare a good application, I just copied and pasted the same application for different scholarships, so in the first place my limited belief directed my lazy action which created bad results.

However, in 2013 I strongly believed that I could achieve an Erasmus scholarship so I made a real effort to prepare for the application and I achieved it. You could argue that I had more experience, but the key factor was I carefully edited and restructured the application, telling my true stories in a powerful careful way. My experience didn't change significantly (I only worked for Samsung since graduation) but my strong desire and empowering beliefs were much more genuine. When scholarship sponsors read an application or interview somebody, they want to see the honesty, confidence and enthusiasm of the person in achieving the scholarship. If you don't event believe in you how can they are confident to believe in you.

Similarly, in 2013 I didn't dare to apply for Chevening because I thought it was harder to achieve compared to Erasmus. At that time, I could not know where that thought came from, but I think probably because the main mission of Erasmus is associated with 'quality higher education academia' – what I have been doing well while that of Chevening is with creating 'future leaders / influencers' – that sounds big. That made me feel I was not one of the 'future leaders / influencers', so I thought Chevening was not for me. This was until 2015, when I was in a position where I completely believed that I could get any scholarships if I wanted to that I could be a leader, of my life first. I applied only for one scholarship (Chevening) that year and I got it.

You may again argue that without the extra two years I wouldn't have obtained a Chevening scholarship. The truth is that there were not many changes in my application for Chevening compared to the application for an Erasmus scholarship (you can refer to the big idea 3 to distinguish between a part of a failing application and a winning application). My goals and my motivations were the same but the main differences were that I dared to apply and I expressed my desire of studying abroad with Chevening scholarship then came back to help Vietnam in a better way. If I would have had the confidence to apply for it two years earlier, I might have won it. We don't know if we don't try. When we try, if we don't get it, we learn from it.

I knew a scholar (Gabriel) who applied for a Chevening scholarship 10 days before the deadline and he achieved it. Gabriel didn't know about the scholarship before, he had been a manager for five years and after a trip to the UK, he fell in love with the country. He went back to Brazil and told himself that he had to find a way to go to the UK. As he searched, he found Chevening, he applied right away even after finding out it was just 10 days before the deadline. It didn't matter if he didn't get it, all he knew was to apply for it. 'You can learn from it if you don't get it, but at least you have to try', he shared with me in our interview. I don't recommend you to wait until the last minute but I urge you not to limit yourself, to have courage and just to give it a try. I also knew some scholars who didn't meet one of the criteria in the scholarship description but they applied for it anyway because their desire was so strong, and most importantly, they didn't mind the failure. They focused on creating the opportunities for themselves not the failure. They focused on learning to move forward rather than not taking action.

Therefore, you must allow yourself to think bigger, to act bigger in order to achieve a bigger goal. You must allow yourself to try to keep learning from the experience. The sooner you try, the sooner you may fail but the sooner you will learn how to succeed.

Call for action:

1. Write down the scholarships that you would like to achieve and ask yourself whether you are limiting yourself with an average scholarship instead of aspiring to a good scholarship. Challenge yourself to strive for what you consider to be the best scholarship and work towards it.

3 scholarships that I am applying are:

...

...

...

If nothing stops me and I have complete permission to choose, 3 scholarships that I want to apply are:

...

...

...

2. Write down the timeline in which you plan to achieve the scholarship. Ask yourself whether you procrastinate because you think you cannot achieve it and wait until a later day. Challenge yourself to decide that today – the moment you have the desire - is the day to start working towards it.

The deadlines of the 3 scholarships that I want to apply are:

...

...

...

If nothing stops me and I have complete permission to choose, 3 deadlines that I want to achieve the scholarships are:

...

...

...

3. Even if you think you don't fit the criteria in the scholarship this year, challenge yourself to apply for it if you really want it. You have nothing to lose but a great experience to learn from. With that, you gain the experience and increase the possibility to achieve the scholarship at the later time of applying.

Recommended books:

1. Think and grow rich - Napoleon Hill

2. The Magic of Thinking Big: David J. Schwartz

Big Idea 3: Your true best self, your competitive advantage of success

> *"Success in any endeavour depends on the degree to which it is an expression of your true self."*
>
> —*Ralph Marston*

Why do you need to be your true best self? The one attribute that only you and no one else has, is your best true self! Among all the candidates, you only need your true and best self to be outstanding. If you pretend to be someone else, you just dismiss your competitive advantage – your uniqueness. Instead of pretending to appear nicely as someone you are not, learn to present your true self authentically. You need to present your true best self genuinely both in paper application as well as in the interview. The motivation letter is the key successful factor to distinguish you from the other candidates. In the motivation letter, scholarship sponsors know whether you are genuinely sharing your thoughts, your desire, your motivations or not. Whether you are embodying your true best self or not will be presented even more clearly in the actual interview. You will probably argue that if everyone is their best self, everyone has a competitive advantage. Yes, that is why you don't want to lose that advantage.

How can you be your true but best self? You just need to tell your story and express your desire to better yourself and make a contribution to people's lives – because it is really the core value of human being since we were born despite different contexts. Think about your life as a story and your purpose or your life goal is the theme of the story. When you share your life story, you want to align all your life events with the theme. Don't copy exactly the motivation letter from others or you will lose your unique life story. If you learn from successful people, you don't learn to be exactly like them but to model their success, their mindset and their strategies, to enhance your best true self. It is also the mission of this book – providing you the mindset of people who have achieved their goals in life rather than giving you their applications or motivations letters – that helps minimize the influence of these examples on your process of self-discovery.

You may also want to include the scholarship application as a milestone in your life story. The milestone of achieving a scholarship should play a role in advancing your life to the next step towards the theme.

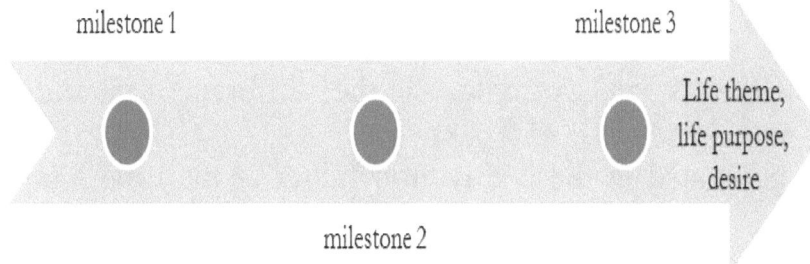

My story started with my childhood desire. I always had a desire to help people around me although I didn't know how. All I knew was that I had to do my best at everything. This desire is the main theme throughout my life story and what I have done has been driven by it. I use the desire as the main theme in any motivation letter. I did not change the core values of it even if I didn't get the scholarship the first time because it has been a part of me. I just learned to present it in a better way with a stronger emotion and beliefs. When I interviewed other scholars, they all shared the same best advice for future scholars 'be honest with yourself.' If all scholars share the same message, you may want to be proud of your best self to gain the competitive advantage over other candidates.

Here is an example of the difference in the vibe generated in the Motivation Letter at the time I failed a scholarship and that at the time I won a scholarship. You can read and think about the difference before reading my analysis.

A part of the introduction (when I failed a scholarship):

I always think I am the person who will change the standard of living of not only my family but also people in my province. According to me, nothing is impossible. "I will become what I think about. No matter how miserable and wonderful the present moment is, the future can be even more fulfilling and joyous". I have a lot of energy and I have clear plans to change the quality of my family's life for better and help other people. I want to inspire others to be their best and make a difference in life.

A part of the introduction (when I won a scholarship):

I have had a burning desire to change the world since I was a small kid. As a kid, I did not know what I would do to change the world, but I did feel that burning desire and I strongly believed I could do it. The feeling got stronger and stronger day by day. More importantly, the

> *way to change the world got clearer and was identified.*
>
> *My mission is to empower the youth in general and in*
>
> *Vietnam in particular to be the leaders of their lives to*
>
> *nonstop loving, living and giving to make a difference in*
>
> *life.*

Do you see the difference between these two styles? Do you find that the information in the two styles is not so different but the vibe is different? In the second piece of writing, my desire is no longer theoretical, but is my real feeling ant that I am living on my mission. I do not need to write 'I have a lot of energy', but you might have noticed that the energy is shown in each strong statement. The belief in my mission is expressed in the statement 'My mission is ...' instead of 'I want to ...', which gives the reader a sense that I have defined the mission in a clear way and acted on it instead of just wanting to do it.

How about you? What's your desire? Set your mind at the state of mind of your best self - the positive self to express that desire, turning that desire into a positive affirmation - into something you are acting on it! Let your best service and growth mindset fire to the reader through each statement of the application!

Call for action:

1. Think about one main theme in your life story which can be your purpose, your desire, the one thing that has guided all of your actions to thrive.

The life goal that I always want to achieve is:

...

2. List different milestones in your life story, make sure you include both activities and emotions in each milestone so people can feel it when they read it.

3 important milestones that have helped me realize my goal are:

...

...

...

3. Practice sharing it with others with empowering emotions.

3 people I want to share my goal and milestones with are:

...

...

...

4. Write it down in the motivation letter with empowering emotions.

Recommended books:

1. Authentic Happiness: Using the New Positive Psychology to Realize Your Potential for Deep Fulfillment_Martin E. P. Seligman

2. Discover Your Authentic Self: Be You, Be Free, Be Happy _Sherrie Dillard

YOUR STRATEGIES

I never thought about strategy the first time I applied for a scholarship but I wish I had done so. If you look at all successful people and companies, they all have a competitive strategy or they made mistakes then they figured it out.

You may ask why do you need to have a strategy to apply only for a scholarship but not for bigger things such as opening a company. Why shouldn't you? It certainly increases your chance of achieving the scholarship by utilising your resources such as knowledge and experience. Why don't you create a good habit of achieving a small goal well so that you can be better at achieving bigger goals in the future? If achieving a scholarship is a big goal in your life, you certainly want to have a competitive strategy for it.

Big Idea 4: The selective rule 80/20, 'the optimizer' of your resources towards success

> *'80% of the effects come from 20% of the causes.'*
>
> — *Pareto principle*

The fundamental idea of the 80/20 rule derives from the fact that the majority of results come from the minority of causes. For example, the majority of money in the world is in the hands of a few. We spend the greater part of our time with only a few people. The 80/20 rule suggests that we can create more good results by performing fewer activities, the activities that matter to our goals. Therefore, you can increase the opportunities of getting a scholarship by selectively applying for fewer scholarships, the scholarships that really matter to your desire and fit with your criteria.

I have considered the 80/20 rule as one of the most effective rules for succeeding in life. When you focus on fewer things, you spread your time and energy on fewer goals. Don't let the quantity influence the quality.

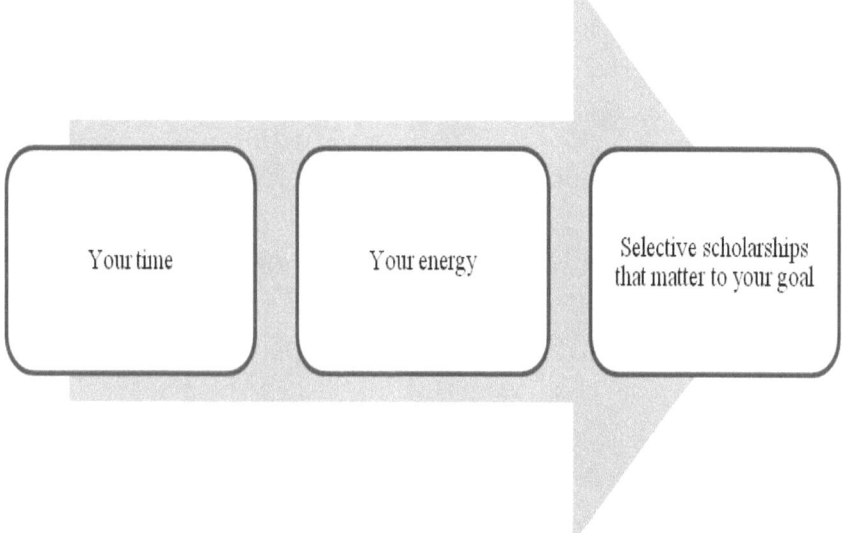

In 2011, I applied for 7 different scholarships. I listened to someone who told me 'You should apply for as many scholarships as possible.' Chasing quantity could lead to a lazy attitude. As I applied for so many different scholarships, I allowed myself to be lazy when I conducted research on each scholarship. I simply copied and pasted the same application to different scholarships.

If I had spent that time and energy on doing serious research on some major scholarships, I would have had a greater possibility of obtaining one of these.

In 2013, I learned from that mistake and applied for only 3 scholarships and obtained 2 of them including Eramus. I carefully conducted research for each scholarship to make sure it met my criteria such as full financial support (even allowing me to save money) or major to study. As I focused on only three scholarships, I couldn't make an excuse not to do this well. The time and energy I spent for seven scholarships now narrowed down to just three scholarships, so being more focused produced better results. Similarly, in 2015, I applied only for a Chevening scholarship with a strong belief that I would get it, I put all of my effort on the application, only Chevening application, and I achieved it. I believe that the fewer scholarships for which we apply, the more focused and serious we are towards achieving them.

If you still believe that the more scholarships you apply for, the more chances you have, then please try to make a serious effort to ensure the best possible quality of each scholarship as you apply for fewer scholarships. The next idea (big idea 5) will guide you to produce your final list of scholarships.

You can also use the 80/20 rule to select your thoughts about applying for a scholarship. There are thoughts that disempower you to apply for a scholarship (e.g. I am not good enough, I am not ready yet. The scholarship is hard so it is not for me. I am not confident). There are also thoughts that empower you (e.g. I am ready to apply for the scholarship. The scholarship is competitive so it is worth applying for so that I can maximise my ability. I am becoming more confident everyday by better developing myself). You can see that it is the empowering thoughts that you want to keep with you.

You are 100 percent capable of controlling your thoughts. You can keep reminding yourself to be selective in choosing the thoughts that come to your mind. You can practice three times a day to redirect disempowering thoughts to empowering thoughts. When you do it often enough, it becomes a part of you and your habit. When doing this regularly, the empowering emotion muscles get stronger and you take action with a positive mindset which means you increase the chance of achieving the scholarship.

Call for Action:

To cultivate your empowering thoughts

1. Write down different thoughts that come to your mind about applying for a scholarship.

Thoughts normally come to my mind when I think about applying for a scholarship are:

...

...

...

...

...

...

2. Divide them into two columns, disempowering thoughts and empowering thoughts.

Positive thoughts include:

...

...

...

Negative thoughts include:

...

...

...

3. Find the antidote for the disempowering thoughts (e.g. 'I am not good enough' becomes 'I am learning to be better every day' so you can allow yourself to start to be great).

The antidotes for negative thoughts include:

...

...

...

4. Associate all the empowering thoughts with getting the scholarship.

3 positive thoughts motivate me best are:

...

...

...

5. Put these thoughts in your phone, laptop, notebook or calendar to keep reminding yourself to focus on them.

3 ways to accumulate positive thoughts are:

...

...

...

6. Using visualisation practice to imagine yourself in the position of achieving the scholarship with all sense and empowering emotions for 5 minutes every morning and before going to bed.

7. Reinforce these positive emotions and beliefs by enhancing any skills needed to achieve the scholarship (e.g, language, writing) (you can refer to the big idea 6 where you can see the suggested daily strategic action to develop essential skills to achieve a goal).

Recommended books:

1. The 80/20 Principle: The Secret of Achieving More with Less_ Richard Koch

2. The 80/20 Manager: Ten Ways to Become a Great Leader _ Richard Koch

YOUR STRATEGIC ACTION MAP

You positioned your MIND in the possession of a scholarship. You had a strong BELIEF that you could obtain it. You knew you should FOCUS only on top scholarships on which you could make a serious EFFORT to conduct research and to prepare for the application. You now need to identify what are the top scholarships on which to focus and the map which will take you from where you are to achieving the scholarships.

Big Idea 5: Your goal statement, the measure of necessary effort to your success

> *'People with goals succeed because they know where they're going.'*
>
> *—Earl Nightingale*

Why your goal statement is important. You need to create a scholarship goal statement to direct and measure how much EFFORT you need to make in order to achieve it. For example, when you apply for a Chevening scholarship, you arguably have to put in more effort compared to an Erasmus scholarship. You have to go for the interview after the application round in Chevening which you don't need to do in an Erasmus scholarship. If you find yourself reading this in the month of June, wanting to apply for a Chevening scholarship, you know that you have around 4 months left to prepare for the application before the deadline (Chevening deadline is often in Nov).

To create a goal statement, you need to identify which scholarship are you going to apply for. Remember, you need to be strategic in selecting only those scholarships that matter most to you (recall the 'big idea 4').

Step 1: Your life goal statement

Achieving a scholarship is just one milestone in your life story so you want to clarify your life goal or your life mission so that you know which role the scholarship plays in your life story. You can see a format and an example of creating your life goal statement below.

Your life goal:

Name:

Date:

In (year:), I (your name:) am (the ideal role for you for example: a social entrepreneurial) who (what impact do you want to make, for example: create jobs) (your audiences, for example: young people).

Signed by: (your name)

An example of my life goal:

In 2018, I, Jen, am a personal development trainer who empowers one millionyoung people to make a difference in their lives.

Signed by: Jenvuhuong 1st January 2017, Bristol, UK

If you are not yet clear about what your life mission is, then you just need to remind yourself about cultivating the growth and service mindsets by continuously developing yourself for the better and contributing as much as you can to life.

Step 2: Your prioritised criteria list

A prioritised criteria list is built on the basis of your life mission, life desire, interests and preferences. You can use the list to evaluate which scholarships you should focus on. You can perform a brainstorm on all the criteria and then prioritise them based on their importance to you.

There are three main areas to create and evaluate a list of criteria:

- Your life MISSION and the scholarship mission. The Chevening scholarship looks for a future leader and influencer. If you are not interested in leading and influencing people and you prefer to do research as a career, you may not feel compelled to apply for the scholarship and may want to look for scholarships in some research universities in Korea such as Chonnam National University.

- Your PREFERENCE (e.g. country, major) and the availability of the scholarship. If you want to study in Europe, Erasmus would be a good scholarship but if you want to study in the USA, Fullbright would be a good choice. If you want freely to choose at which university to study and want to study in the UK, Chevening gives you that chance.

- Your RESOURCES (e.g. GPA, English certificate, nationality) and your willingness to make an effort and the scholarship's requirements. If you apply for a Chevening scholarship, you need to be willing to compete with other candidates both from your own country and from all over the world.

Based on the three main areas, you can create a detailed list of criteria when you choose to apply for a scholarship. I would recommend that the list has about five to ten criteria. You can then evaluate each criterion in order, according to its importance as in the table below.

Your prioritised list of criteria to select a scholarship	Evaluation for each criterion(why it is important)
1.	
2.	
3.	
4.	
5.	
6.	
7.	
8.	
9.	
10.	

The following table shows you an example of my prioritised list and the evaluation of the importance of each criterion.

Prioritised list of criteria from which to choose a scholarship	Evaluation for each criterion (why it is important)
1. Is it a full scholarship or not? If yes, how much should it be?	Yes, it should be a full scholarship because I would never let my family or myself pay for further studying and I believe I deserve to get it as I have studied hard and have had a strong desire to help others. It should be at least 1000 Euros per month to cover expenses and allows some savings.
2. Am I eligible to apply (in terms of nationality etc.) because some scholarships only accept people from particular countries?	To make sure of not focusing on the wrong scholarship or wrong framework (however, remember you can give it a try if you want it so badly, you feel that you would regret if you don't give it a try, so just do it and learn from it to move on).
3. Is it ok to be committed to work for anyone after finishing the course?	There should be no commitment. If there is, it should still allow me to follow my mission.
4. Which degree do you want to	Only one year, only master's (because I

study?	want to focus on starting my own business before studying PhD).
5. In which country do you want to study?	European countries so I can travel to discover different countries in Europe.
6. In which language do you want to study?	English language as I want to develop my training career internationally.
7. What are the skills you need to achieve your life goal?	Networking in foreign countries as I want to develop my training career internationally.
8. Which majors build up these skills, and are the chances of building them in the place you study are high or low?	Related to international management. Apart from my school, the place I study need to have active community to develop entrepreneurship and soft-skills.
9. Does the university need to be famous or just need to be good at the course that you are looking for?	Not necessary to be famous if all the above categories are fit.
10. Which location?	Not necessary to be famous if all the above categories are fit.

Step 3: List of potential scholarships

Based on your prioritised criteria list, you can use the filter functions in any scholarship website to obtain the extracted list of scholarships that are suitable to your criteria. For example, if you want to study master's, you can choose this category in a scholarship site to see all the possible options:

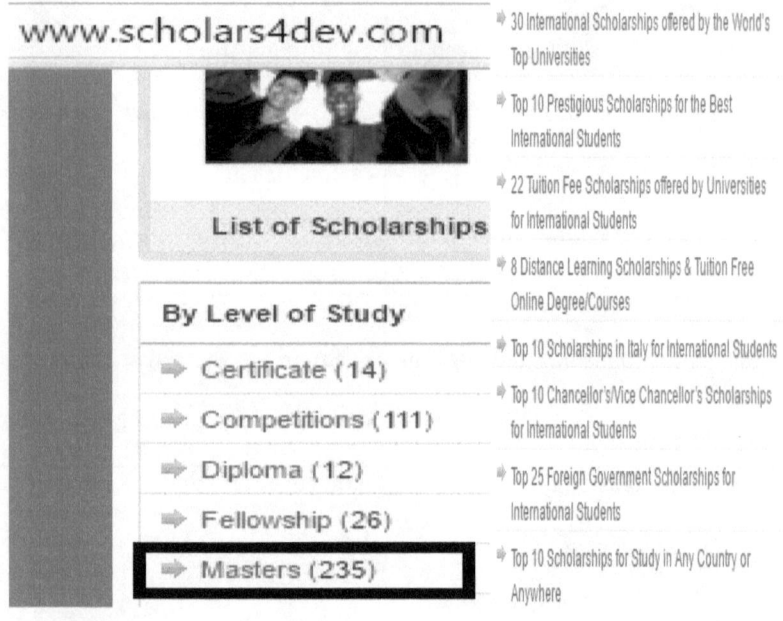

You can use some sources for searching scholarships as in the table below. I would recommend to search for not more than 5 scholarships (remember, you don't want to go for quantity and lose quality). You should use English to have access to more scholarships.

Sources	Details
Google search	Use some keywords like 'Full scholarships in the UK' or be more specific like 'Full scholarships in the UK for Vietnamese' and so on if you want to study in the UK.
Popular sites	Search, subscribe to keep updated scholarship information from the scholarship sites: http://www.scholars4dev.com/ https://www.findaphd.com/ http://scholarshippoints.com/ http://scholarships.com/ http://www.chegg.com/ http://fastweb.com/ https://www.cappex.com/
Social network	Facebook, Twitter (using keywords to search for the groups), YouTube For example: https://www.facebook.com/jenvuhuonglovelivegive/ https://www.youtube.com/c/JenVuHuong
Embassy websites	Website of embassies of the countries where you want to study Websites of the scholarships if you have already heard about them For example, Chevening scholarship: http://www.chevening.org/
Network	Former scholars, successful friends, trustworthy relatives,

	teachers (I would even consider it would be the first source to consult but you then still need to compare information from different sources)
Your universities	International departments
Events	Scholarship events, TV education shows
Centers	Scholarship agency, language centres (I would consider these are last choices if I aim to full scholarships because they normally advise for partly scholarships or full scholarships but only for tuition fee or a little bit living expense support)

My favourite site is http://www.scholars4dev.com/ because they have a clear interface, frequently updated scholarships, and they also keep categories(e.g. top scholarships to study in the UK as shown in the screen capture above).

Step 4: Build a prioritised scholarship list

After choosing a maximum of 5 scholarships, you can now use the prioritised criteria list to evaluate each scholarship according to your own criteria. You then can weight each scholarship on a scale of 0 to 5 (0: completely not satisfied, 1: really not satisfied; 2: not really satisfied, 3: quite satisfied, 4: really satisfied, 5: completely satisfied). Then, on the basis of the total scores, you can choose the scholarships with the highest scores.

Your final list of chosen scholarships should not be more than three. Remember the 80/20 rule - getting better results by doing fewer things – the things that matter.

Prioritised criteria (S: Scholarship)	S1 (Scale 0 to 5)	S2 (Scale 0 to 5)	S3 (Scale 0 to 5)	S4 (Scale 0 to 5)	S5 (Scale 0 to 5)
1. Is it a full scholarship or not? If yes, how much should it be?					
2. Am I eligible to apply (in terms of nationality etc. because some scholarships only					

accept people from certain countries?				
3. Whether the commitment that the scholarship requires me to do influence my life mission?				
4. Which degree do you want to study for?				
5. In which country do you want to study?				
6. In which language do you want to study?				
7. Which skills do you need to achieve your life goal?				
8. Which majors build up these skills, and are the chances of building them in the place				

you study high or low?					
9. Does the university need to be famous or just need to be good at the course that you are looking for?					
10. Whether the location is convenient for transport and has a nice neighbourhood?					
Total scores					
Chosen scholarship					

Step 5: Translate your life goal statement to a scholarship goal statement

Once you decide which scholarship to apply for, you need to make it exist in the real world by creating a scholarship goal statement. Remember that this is linked to your life goal. Think about it as one step nearer to your life goal.

> **Scholarship goal statement**
>
> Name:
>
> Date:
>
> In (month, year:), I (name:) will get (for example: Chevening scholarship) which helps me to raise my standards to help more people in a greater way.
>
> Signed by:

You need to sign your goal statement to show your commitment. Think about why companies want to sign a contract with you. They need you to show them your commitment! So you also need to commit with your own goal!

Step 6: How to evaluate a good goal

Apart from aligning with your life goal or your growth and service mindset, a goal works best when it is challenging. If the goal is easy, you don't feel motivated to maximise your resources. Remember, you need to think big for yourself because you deserve it and you can do it. Moreover, a goal also needs to be specific (date and place) where you know how much effort you need to apply yearly, monthly, weekly, and daily to achieve your goal.

Step 7: Turning the goal into practical action and results

After creating the goal statement, you need to teach your brain to engage with the goal that motivates you to take practical action to achieve it. Therefore, you need to see your goal in the real world by writing it in your notebook, phone or laptop. You also need to use visualisation to feel the goal everyday, to turn it into practical action and then into results. If you don't see and feel it with your mind first, your brain doesn't know what to 'tell' your physical body to do in order to achieve it.

Just think about the process of going to buy an ice cream: you tell yourself that you want it and you will feel happy when you eat it, which triggers your action 'going to buy the ice cream'. All your actions come from your thoughts either to gain pleasure or avoid pain. Knowing that, you can tell yourself what pleasure you can have when winning the scholarship, see it and feel it with all the senses of your body.

The following steps will guide you to turn your goal into practical and continuous action:

- Write the goal in your notebook, business card or a sticker then put it into your wallet;

- Create a picture with your goal then set it as your desktop and phone wallpaper;

- Set an alarm to remind yourself to connect with your goal daily;

- Visualising that when you wake up everyday, you work towards achieving the scholarship until the moment you receive the acceptance letter, and then enjoy studying abroad. It is important to involve emotions when you visualise as well as the moments when you overcome struggles that teach your brain never to give up;

- Share with others to keep the accountability and motivation (sharing with people who trust in you and your dream);
- Take at least three actions each day to turn the goal into results (the next section will identify which actions to take).

Recommended books:

1. 7 Habits of Highly Effective People _ Stephen Covey

2. Goals _ Brian Tracy

YOUR STRATEGIC DAILY ACTION

Big Idea 6: Your effective action plan, the road of your success

> 'The path to success is to take massive, determined
>
> action'
>
> —Tony Robbins

You have already decided which scholarship you want to achieve. You have already created your scholarship goal statement to identify when you want to achieve the scholarship. You have already made your goal, now existing in the real world, by writing it on paper or adding it to your laptop or phone, as well as in your mind and your body by visualisation with emotions. You now need to take daily action to make it happen.

Step 1: Know the rules of the game

We sometimes love breaking the rules because it can create novelty and innovation. However, there are some basic rules that we must first follow if we are at least to enter the game eligibly, then we can express our creativity and innovation. Nevertheless, there are exceptions. Don't let the rules stop you but let them motivate you.

If you truly want to get a scholarship, even if the basic written 'rules' or what you call 'requirements' show that you are not eligible, just give it a try. For example, if the scholarship says you need to have a GPA higher than 7/10 and your actual GPA is lower than that, just apply but if you don't get it then work on improving your GPA, then apply again. Remember that I previously shared the fact that some scholars didn't meet the requirements written on the website of some scholarships, but they applied anyway and they got it. The reason is because they knew that they had a strong desire and they knew that if they didn't apply, they would not obtain it; but by applying they created the possibility of achieving it. And they also proactively attended different activities to develop other strengths to compensate for their low GPA. If you have a strong desire, don't let anything stop you and don't let the fear of rejection stop you. Let it motivate you to work on yourself then attract the scholarship that you want. That is why, in the previous section, I didn't put much emphasis on the criteria of the requirements of any scholarship because I didn't want them to stop your ambition.

There are normally four primary requirements for any full scholarships:

- GPA greater than 7/10
- Two recommendation letters
- IELTS/TOEFL/English certificate (e.g. Ielts at least 6.5 or 7.0)
- Motivation letter

You can create a table to list all the requirements and notes for your chosen scholarships.

Details	Scholarship 1	Scholarship 2	Scholarship 3
Major			
Country to study			
Opening date and deadline			
Requirements			
Other notes			

Step 2: Identify your action plan

Once you have already identified the requirements of a scholarship - your goal; you need to create an action plan in order to achieve the goal. Setting a goal is important but to achieve it, you need to take it seriously and take real action, regularly, steadily, moment by moment, day by day, and then you can achieve it.

Why having an action plan is important

- To identify what activities you need to do every day, every week, every month to get closer to your goals

- To keep you on track

- To keep you focused on things that matter to your goals

- To check your progress in celebrating and keeping your momentum

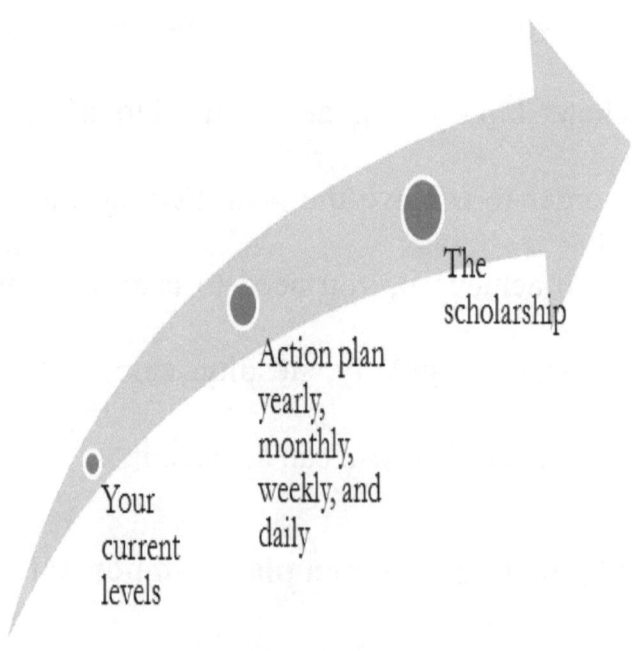

The scholarship

Action plan yearly, monthly, weekly, and daily

Your current levels

How to create the action plan

- Identify your current levels according to the criteria of your chosen scholarships (GPA, recommendation letters, English certificate, and motivation letter).

- Compare your current levels and the scholarships' requirements to identify the gaps between your current levels and the required levels (e.g. you have Ielts 6.0 but the scholarship requires Ielts 7.0 so you just need to close 1 score gap to meet the requirement).

- Identify how many months remain before the deadlines of the scholarships.

- Identify the monthly action plan to improve your current levels to meet the scholarship requirements.

- Keep checking the improvement process to adjust.

Your definite action plan Name: ; Date:				
Current time	1stweek	2ndweek	3rdweek	4th week
Time left				
Current level and level required by the scholarship				
Actions to close the gap between current level and scholarship's requirement				
Starting time				
Progressing check	Improved? How much?	Improved? How much?	Improved? How much?	Improved? How much?
3 things to improve				

Step 3: Win English requirement

The following illustrates an example of the current English level of scholar named Ben (my favourite English name) and Ben's action plan to achieve the required English level.

Step 4: Win GPA requirement

The following is an example of identifying your current GPA and action plan to improve GPA to meet the scholarship's requiremen

Your definite action plan

Name: Ben; Date: 7 June 2017

Deadline/Time left: 3 months

Requirement GPA 7.7/10

Your current level: 7.5/10

You need to identify:

- Which subjects have the potential to improve your GPA?
- How can you increase your score? Spending more time? Asking friends for help? Asking teachers for help? Learning from online courses? Just choose a way then take action upon it to see which one works the best for you or maybe combines them together
- If your GPA is equal to or higher than the scholarship requirement, you may still want to work on maintaining or improving it to enhance your competitive advantage

Details	Subject 1	Subject 2	Subject 3
Daily action	Reading	Consulting friends	Consulting tutors
Others	Establishing group work	Attending group work	Attending online course
Progress check after 3 weeks	Improved? How much?	Improved? How much?	Improved? How much?
3 things to do to improve			

Step 5: Obtain recommendation letters

Recommendation letters are meant to be written by people who have worked with you, such as your supervisors, tutors, lecturers and previous managers. The letters are meant to highlight their impressions and experiences when working with you. Fundamentally, the letters are intended to highlight your strengths so that scholarship sponsors have enough evidence to consider whether to offer you the scholarship or not. This may be the step which is a struggle for future scholars because they think they have no one to ask for **a** recommendation letter. The truth is that you are scared of rejection or have not put in any effort to give your values to the people who can give you recommendation letters. Keep in mind two principles regarding recommendation letters: ask genuinely for help and be willing to make an effort to add values to others. The following steps will guide you in the process of obtaining recommendation letters.

- Make a list of all the people who are potentially available for you to reach and ask for recommendation letters and then put them in different categories: industry, working experiences, position, expertise and over what period of time they have known you.

Social network	Contact list	How long they have known you	Industry	Positions	Expertise	Prioritised
University						
Work						
Local community						
Influencers						

- Remember the 80/20 rule, focusing on the relationships that matter most instead of all relationships; you want to prioritise them based on:

  - The relevance of the areas in which they work and the major or skills that scholarships require (for example, if you apply for a Chevening scholarship, you need to contact people who can praise your leadership skills. If you argue that you don't have anyone yet, look for the opportunity to start working for someone, even a part-time job either online or offline, and then tell your stories of managing the job).

    (you can join our volunteer team to do leadership projects at jenvuhuong.com/betheleaders)

  - The most recent year is the best.

- Pick up each area (e.g. work, academic), one person is the best in each area.

- Again, it is important to study the areas that are relevant to the scholarships and those are able to highlight your strengths or potentials in these areas. If you are close enough to the professors, you could ask them to adjust to outline specific skills. However, I believe it is best to be genuine (remember the big idea 3 – be your best true self).

How to approach the professors/managers:

If you express your sincere wish, the reason WHY you want to go abroad to study, there is very few successful person who would refuse to help you. Imagine you are successful in life, do you reject giving a recommendation to your student or employee who has a desire to better themselves and make a contribution to life? If you have not made enough contributions for them to write a recommendation letter, ask them to give you more time to do that. You can ask for specific requirements about what you need to do to get the letters.

Don't tell yourself the story that they would not help you. Tell yourself 'I will give it a try and do whatever it takes to get it.' If they still reject you despite your effort to give values, ask someone else. I remember I didn't dare to ask one of my tutors to write a letter for me since I thought he didn't remember who I was as he taught me for only one semester. However, the more I thought about my desire of going abroad, the more I found it greater than any fear of rejection. Therefore, I knew that if I didn't try, I would regret it later. I then emailed him and he immediately emailed me to arrange a meeting and to hear more about what I was looking for from the recommendation letter. You see, you can't really assume things without taking real ACTION first.

Keep in mind the step where most people fail is to not even try to ASK:

- Just ask for help because everyone needs help in life.

- Ask, don't assume they will reject.

- Even if they reject, ask again what else you can do to have their help or ask others until you find 'right people'.

- Know that the 'right people', who are supportive, will be glad to give you a hand. No 'right people' deny helping someone to realise their dreams and to know whether someone is the right one to help you or not, you need to ASK first.

(You can ask me at jenvuhuong.com/thegoalachiever)

Structures of a recommendation letter:

Here is my suggested structure for a recommendation letter:

Recommendation letter	
Headline	Name of reference
	Position
	Office address
	Logo
Opening	To whom it may concern
	How/when/related to how the referee knows you?
Body	Develop the process of your improvement/contribution
	Difficulties that you overcome
	Highlight your strong points/achievements
	Your potential to develop in the future
Conclusion	Highlight the referee's beliefs in your ability that deserves to get the scholarship/to step up in life
	Express the willingness to be contacted for further concerns

Step 6: Your outstanding motivation letter

Why a motivation letter is important: A motivation letter is the key to making you outstanding within yourself and among others candidates who meet the other three primary requirements (GPA, English, recommendation letters) of a scholarship. If you follow the previous ideas in this book and emotionally attach yourself to them, it is likely that you love writing a motivation letter and you should not have any struggles with it.

How to write an outstanding motivation letter: A motivation letter will let the scholarship sponsors make a decision by answering the fundamental question: 'Why you but not others?' You may wonder if you need to be a star. Do you need to be someone else? The absolute answer is NO! You just need to be your TRUE BEST self. Remember the section, 'Big Idea 3'. You just need to hold on to your life story, your true self, your uniqueness, your desire, your life purpose and your life goal. You just need to stand out by bringing out your true and best self. I firmly believe the key success factor of my application in all scholarships that I achieved was my true story about continuous action to achieve my childhood desire of bettering my family and other people's lives. According to the big idea 3, you can consider your dream or your mission as the string of your development journey since you were a kid, you then can select the milestones to clarify the motivation and realisation process of your dream or your mission.

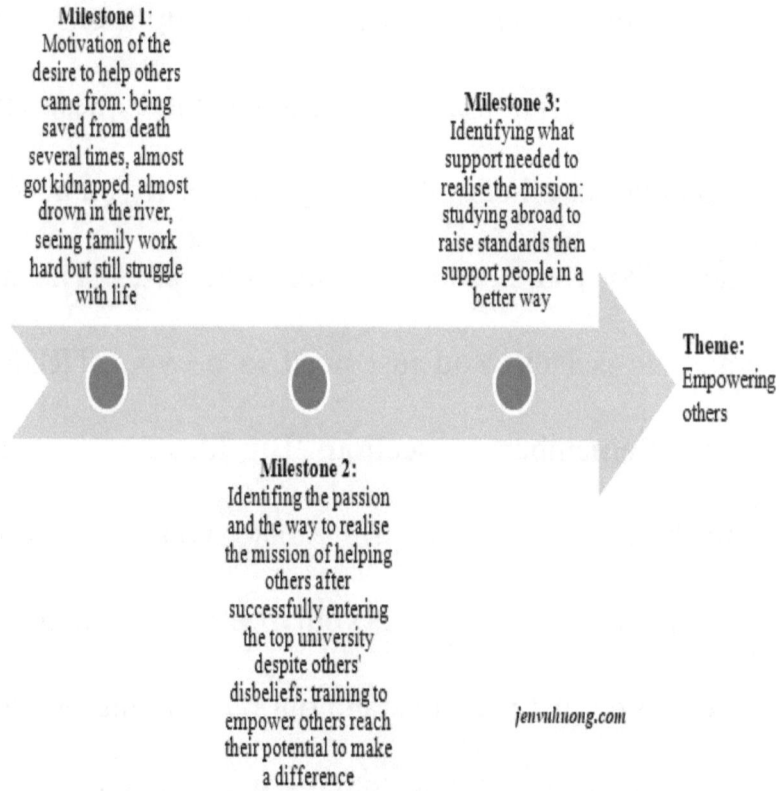

Raising a clear plan to realise the dream is also an important point in the Motivation letter. If you show people your target – where you want to go – but not the way to go their, they will get lost and you don't want to make the scholarship sponsors feel lost on your life plan. One of the differences between the time I failed a scholarship and the time I achieved it is the clarity and specificity of my action plan to realise my goal. As I shared before, at the beginning of my journey in applying for a scholarship, I referred a lot from the internet so I didn't use much my critical thinking to identify a clear plan matching with my potential and passion. In those first Motivation letters (the times I didn't get a scholarship), I just shared generally that I wanted to go abroad to develop myself then came back to Vietnam to share my experience with others. In the Motivation letters that I won scholarships, I clearly clarified my action plan. For example, in one year after coming back to Vietnam, I would open a community to gather both Vietnamese and foreigners to share ideas and develop skills/mindset and in 3 years, the community would be expanded to the whole country. I also emphasied that the experience and knowledge that I have learned about International Management (my chosen major) would help me run the community effectively. Hence, you need to critically ask yourself what values that you may receive in the studying abroad journey and what are their roles in the journey of realising your mission.

The following part will help you imagine about the flow of connecting between your mission and the action plan to realise it.

Structure

Here is my suggestion for the motivation letter's structure:

Motivation letter		
Structures	Main points	Suggestions
Introductio n	Highlight your lifelong mission/passion	Make a good impression
		Be genuine
		Be ambitious
		Express a growth and service mindset
		Express your enthusiasm and willingness to take action

Body	Tell your life stories with the main milestones	Explain how these stories relate to your mission/passion in life
	Breakdown into different paragraphs according to the milestones	Make it specific and relevant
	Highlight the current situations/difficulties towards realising your mission/passion. Highlight the scholarships that should help you to overcome the problems or boost the process of realising your dreams faster	Make it specific and say why the scholarship you are applying for, rather than other scholarships, will help you
	Even though you don't get scholarships, you will still work on realising your dreams	This is excellent and I think it will make you stand out because you are the leader of your life. You will always find a way for any situation, but it would be better to be supported from a good opportunity like having the scholarship
	Your plan after getting the scholarships	This is a really important point because it reflects the return investment of the scholarship sponsor which is mentioned in the 'Big idea 1'. You need to have a service mindset that you want to contribute to life and your plan to achieve the goal is really promising
Conclusion	Sum up the reasons why you are the right one for the scholarship	

Recommended books:

1. Wellness Recovery Action Plan_ Mary Ellen Copeland

2. Think and grow rich - Napoleon Hill

YOUR STRATEGIC PERSISTENCE

Big Idea 7: Your persistence, your self-discipline, the vehicle of your success

> 'Ambition is the path to success, persistence is the vehicle you arrive in.'
>
> — William Eardley IV

Why persistence is important: Life is an up-and-down process rather than a linear one. There are low points where you don't feel motivated and things never seem to work out. The fact is that these low points are just steps in the process of preparing yourself for a new spur. If you are not persistent enough, you give up before reaching these spurring points, therefore you give up before reaching your success point.

To overcome the moments when you don't feel motivated, you can remind yourself of the reason and the desire that made you decide to apply for the scholarship in the first place. Remember your goal, and that your purpose is bigger than any struggle. Remember how badly you want to achieve them. Remember you have already started, so there is no reason to stop. You just need to keep moving forward. Each time you fail, remember to learn from the experience in order to improve. Don't repeat the same ways of doing things and expect to get different results.

How to stay persistent? You need to discipline your thoughts to take action everyday to move towards your goals. Your thoughts lead to your actions, and your actions in turn will lead to your results. There will be moments when you may have some disempowering thoughts like 'I am not good enough' or 'I am not ready yet' or 'I am too tired to do it' or 'It is so hard'. These thoughts do not empower you, nor do you want to be a victim of them. Remember, you have 100% control of your THOUGHTS ('big idea 4'). You just need to train them.

Think about what can you do in order to gain more muscle strength. The absolute answer is you need to train your muscles more often. When you go to the gym and do exercises, your muscles get stronger. This is similar to your thoughts' muscle. You can train the thoughts' muscle.

To train the 'thoughts' muscle', you need to create the 'gym' for it by creating habits for your thoughts.

- **Habit 1 - Take control of your morning:** When you wake up in the morning, tell yourself immediately that you are going to take control of your day. You can then spend 20 minutes reading personal development books in English materials (see the list of recommended books at the end of each 'big idea' in this book, or you can read this book again). You can spend 20 more minutes to plan for exercise, 20 minutes to plan your day, five minutes for VISUALISATION about how grateful and happy you will feel when you overcome difficulties to achieve your goal. Do not respond to emails or social media because you first need to invest in yourself and feed your mind with empowering thoughts and action. When you do this, you shall have the momentum to knock down all the tasks during the day.

- **Habit 2 - Complete three important tasks:** **Complete three important tasks** towards your goal during the day in order to keep the momentum. For example, approaching a person can help you write motivation letters and write the first paragraph of your motivation letter then write one essay to prepare for your English exam.

- **Habit 3: Turn defeat into success:** No matter what happens during your day, keep using the mantra 'What can I learn from it?' 'What can I do differently?' 'How can I help people more?' These questions change your focus to the growth and service mindset to move towards your goal always.

- **Habit 4: Keep a gratitude journal**: Before you go to sleep, allow yourself to connect with your soul, to have a deep sleep, by writing your gratitude journal, which is what you feel thankful for on that day. You can also write a journal about your scholarship journey in order to see how much progress you have made.

- **Habit 5: Bring joy to your journey**: The ultimate goal is to gain pleasure by achieving your goal so you want to enjoy everyday.

To support your training process, you can use three powerful reminders:

- **Set up an alarm** or reminder on your phone that you need to do these habits, so that when the alarm sounds, you know you need to stick to it.

- **Put reminders** on small cards and put them in the case of your laptop or wallet, so that when you see them you know you need to stick to your empowering habits.

- **Have an accountable partner**, a person who has the same goal or your mentor (refer to the next section).

Recommended books:

1. Grit: The Power of Passion and Perseverance _ Angela Duckworth

2. Think and grow rich - Napoleon Hill

Big Idea 8: Sharing, work with others toward success

'The best way to multiply your success is to share it with

others.'

—Jen vuhuong

Why is sharing important? If you share your desire of achieving a scholarship with others who have the same desire, with your mentors or with people who have achieved what you are aiming for, then you increase the possibility of achieving the scholarship through the power of collective knowledge and action. When you share your desire, you verbally reinforce your beliefs in that desire of achieving what you want. Moreover, you can be encouraged by others to reinforce your beliefs in being able to achieve your goal. You can also learn from other perspectives to improve your application or yourself.

This means you also want to CHOOSE the right people to share your desire with. You should choose people who are positively driven and passionate, people who have growth and a service mindset, people who trust you and also trust in your potential. Knowing that, you also need to be supportive and respectful of the dreams and goals of others. Remember to treat people as you want to be treated yourself. Remember that when you support others, you can learn from them and from yourself. The success of the person you support is also your success. Your own success is also the success of the person who supports you. Collaboration is the key to growth and success.

Whom to share with: You need to share your dream with the people who believe in your best self, your dream, your desire. The reason you share your dream is to take action towards it instead of giving up on it.

Therefore, you only want to share your dream with people who encourage you to take action to turn the impossible to be possible rather than sharing with those who direct you to the impossible.

Do you still remember the story that I shared my desire of going abroad by getting a full scholarship with a 'not right person' (a senior student in my university and never studied abroad before) and a 'right person' (my tutor who travelled and studied all over Europe). One person (not right person) made me minimize myself, one person (right person) made me believe in myself and took action to realize my goal of achieving a scholarship. Just imagine, if you studied abroad before, experiencing the process of making an effort to apply for a scholarship, then someone later asked you that if they could achieve the scholarship, what would be your answer? Chances you would encourage them because you have been in the same journey and you would feel fulfilled if you would help them to do the same as you did. You also can imagine that if you are a successful person – achieving different goals in life and then someone asks you that whether they would achieve their dream – chances you would encourage them to do it.

Hence, you want to share your dream with those who already achieved the scholarships that you want to apply for or people who are successful and make a certain impact in life or people who trust in your unlimited power – always encourage you to take action to turn the impossible become possible.

If you have someone who has empowered you in your life, express your gratitude to that person by empowering and supporting others. I truly believe that this is the only way for us to move further in life. As the saying goes, 'If you go alone, you go faster; if you go together, you go further - your choice.' I believe that if we have experience of anything in life, we can help others on the same journey. By doing this, we can reinforce our experience and aspire to develop ourselves for the better. This is the reason why I wrote this book, simply to share what I have learned during my journey to inspire you - the future leaders who help me to understand what else I need to improve and to contribute more.

Call for action:

1. Write down the list of the people whom you admire (e.g. your growth friends, your lecturers, your bosses)

3 people who I want to learn from are:

...

...

...

2. Challenge yourself to share with them your desire to apply for a scholarship to get their perspectives and encouragement

3 schedules that I will share my goal with these people are:

...

...

...

3. Reach out to any friends who are also applying for a scholarship to encourage and support them if they need help

3 people who are also applying for the similar scholarships are:

...

...

...

4. Create a group of friends to work towards achieving the scholarship

3 scholarship communities that I will set up or attend are:

...

...

...

Recommended books:

1. Law of Success: An Introduction to the Mastermind, a Definite Chief Aim, Self-Confidence, the Habit of Saving _ Napoleon Hill

2. Think and grow rich - Napoleon Hill

Big Idea 9: Giving, the key of success in the interview winning rule

"We make a living by what we get. We make a life by what we give."

— *Winston S. Churchill.*

Giving is the soul of living_jenvuhuong.com

Congratulations, you have gone through the first round (if the scholarship, such as Chevening, requires an interview). Even if the scholarship does not have an interviewing round, this idea can help you develop a winning mindset for any interview in life either a job interview or in an interview to help you to improve yourself.

Remember to give yourself credit if you have reached this point. Just call a friend to go out to celebrate or do something that you really like such as hiking. Remember, if you don't celebrate small wins, your brain does not know what is good or bad. If it is a big win for you, you need to celebrate even more. Up to this point, there is nothing to stop you as you have equipped yourself with your best. You should have no problem in entering the interview. However, it can be the most frightening step in your scholarship journey because you have to face real people. Therefore, you may think that 'having an interview is terrifying', which is what society has always told us. Up to this point, the interview may make you feel the most doubtful about yourself and your ability to succeed. Nevertheless you know that you can use one simple powerful rule to eliminate the doubts, the fear and the nervousness is to be at your best in the interview by asking yourself 'What meaning do you want to GIVE into the interview?' Scary thoughts or exciting thoughts?

Use this question as a mantra to change all of your doubts and nervousness in order to turn into action towards success. Ask yourself if you want to give the impression that you are nervous during the interview. Do you want to give the impression that you are afraid during the interview? The absolute answer is NO. You want to present your best true self, your powerful story. When you ask these questions, you interrupt the doubts, the fear and the nervousness, then you choose the empowering meaning you want to give to the interview.

Now you are probably wondering how you can do that. Just do a small exercise, ask yourself 'What meaning do I want to GIVE to a meeting with my best friend who has always encouraged me when I have shared the excitement I have felt about my plan to go abroad?' The absolute answer is excitement and your true self.

Maybe you get the idea now! It is your option to choose between GIVING disempowering meanings or empowering meanings to the interview. No matter what your choice is, it does not change the interview by its definition but changes your behaviour and then the result that you want to achieve. So you want to tell yourself the exciting feeling of going abroad to study to achieve your goal to give back to life later. Imagine going to the interview as though you are going to see a supportive friend who is looking forward to hearing about your exciting plan to go abroad and then to move closer to your life goal! If you can just be yourself with your friend, they will buy into the idea and have courage to do it even you are nervous, they will cheer you up and buy into the idea. They will be ready to give you the scholarship as they can see the enthusiasm and potential in your story.

In any question of the interview, always ask yourself what is the empowering meaning you want to GIVE to it.

Below is an example of one interview question in a Chevening interview and the process of giving empowering meaning to it. You want to know why they ask the question and how to create the empowering meaning to the question.

Question: Demonstrate your leadership potential?

Why is the question? The goal of Chevening or any scholarship is to 'develop global leaders', they need to have the 'right' people.

Your empowering meaning to the question:

1. Believe that everyone has the ability to be a leader. Everyone is at least a leader of their own life. The only difference is how much one displays it. Research and history have proved that in order for a person to lead others well, he or she needs to lead himself or herself first. Therefore, you can share in the interview how well you have handled your own life. One scholar shared with me his experience in leading his life in response to this question (and yes, he achieved the scholarship). Do not underestimate some of your experiences of leading a project, life, or a group.

2. You have a desire of becoming a leader to lead others to make a difference to their lives. You can now share what being a

global leader actually means to you. Remember, everything starts with a desire. If you have a desire, you can find a way to develop it. That is why Chevening is looking for 'future leaders'. You can develop this towards the future.

3. Leaders are created not born. Read and learn from great leaders and practice the mindset and behaviours that you want to develop for yourself. You can then share the learning and practice leadership with scholarship sponsor.

The day you receive your acceptance letter from the scholarship, do not forget to congratulate yourself and do not forget to GIVE BACK to the scholarship by making the best out of the experience to GIVE BACK to society. When you focus on GIVING, you go beyond yourself, you live up to your service mindset ('big idea 1') which makes a difference in life.

This book is an act of my thanks GIVING back to the scholarships that I have achieved and my thanks GIVING to you, future scholars, future leaders who will contribute to make the world better place. I believe in you and in your desire to make a difference in life. I believe you can decide to give your best to life everyday. Also I believe that you can decide to give life your kindness everyday. I believe that you can decide to give life your gratitude everyday. I believe that you can decide to give the scholarship thanks for supporting you on the journey towards your mission.

Today is the day for you to be grateful for life and to GIVE your best effort to turn your desire into reality. Everyday. You can do it!

Recommended book:

1. Non-stop loving, living, and giving _Jenvuhuong

2. Unleash your passion _Jenvuhuong

More steps?

Yes, non-stop actions daily toward your life mission.

I truly believe that if you have read my texts up to this point, you are on your way.

Just stay motivated to work on your goals every day. Be disciplined. Enjoy the journey.

It is now just a matter of time.

The universe will answer your quest in a positive way because you deserve it. See you in the community of scholars, most importantly leaders to empower others to make a difference in life.

Today is the day for you!

Non-stop living, loving and giving

Love with respects,

Check out coming books and courses at jenvuhuong.com/thegoalachiever

Thanks message to the readers

The day when you receive your final acceptance letter for your scholarship, GIVE yourself a moment to congratulate yourself for your effort. Take a moment to extract the pattern of success, the 'whats' and 'hows' that have helped you to achieve the scholarship. Pass this knowledge on to others. Let's multiply your success by sharing its patterns. Congratulations, you have just gone through a journey of creating your success roadmap.

If you do not get the offer. You have passed through the journey of learning. Please allow you to let it go, and reflect upon it after some days when you feel better. Set a goal and action plan and act. You can do it again! You can!

When you finish this book, if you only want to take away one message to share with others, it is GIVING. Giving your best at what you do. Giving your values to the scholarship. Giving your gift to make a difference in the world.

Giving, the secret I learned from my siblings that made me find a true reason for living, every moment of life.

If you want to choose only one book in the list of recommended books, it is I CAN DO IT. The book that made me find a map for living a life with meaning and fulfilment.

Stay motivated and make a difference every day.

This is your time. Today is the day to be non-stop living, loving and giving to achieve more!

Talk to you soon!

Jen,

Gratitude moment

I am deeply grateful for my life's different golden tickets. This book is dedicated to my family and the mission of empowering the best version in you to make a difference in life. I wake up every morning grateful that I am alive, with the vibrancy of nonstop living, loving, and giving that is inspired by my family. Despite the distance and time, my heart is always with my family.

To Camilo and Sophie, I cannot express how much thankful and appreciative to your effort and time to edit and share ideas to improve the book. Without you, the publishing book journey would have not been going well.

Stuart Doughty, Tony Robbins, and Brendon Burchard also deserve a great appreciation for inspiring me to share my message and stay in the journey of empowering people to make a difference in their lives.

I could not express how much appreciative I feel toward Erasmus scholarship and Chevening scholarship which gave me the chance to study in Spain and the UK respectively to raise my academic and professional standard that is a great foundation for this book.

Last but not least, I truly appreciate all the participants who are SME's business owners, scholars of Chevening program and leaders of Toastmasters International in all over the world.

It is impossible to thank each and a single person I have met in my life who has inspired me to live with passion every moment of life, so I apologize to all my friends not listed here. I truly appreciate you.

About the Author

Jen Vuhuong (her full Vietnamese name is Vu Thi Huong) obtained a degree in Electronics and Telecommunications from Hanoi University of Science and Technology in Vietnam, an excellent master's degree in Business Innovation and Technology Management in Spain, and an excellent master's degree in International Management in the UK.

After being awarded a scholarship by Samsung Corporation in her final year at university, Jen dedicated two years to work for Samsung Electronics Vietnam as a project owner and an on-the-job trainer. In 2013, she went to Spain for her first master's degree with the world's top full scholarship—Erasmus. In 2014, she moved to work in Malaysia for a Dell partner for almost two years. In 2016, Jen devoted five months to work as an event manager for a bicycle and educational campaign of a Belgian NGO in Vietnam. Later, Jen went to the UK and completed her second master's. Jen went back to Vietnam and participated in different education projects as a trainer, education development manager, business consultant and head of committee of Hanoi Entrepreneur Community. Jen is also the founder of different leadership programs 'Be the Leaders', 'EmpowerYou academy', 'CSpeaking gym' and 'Start with Green'. Jen has recently worked with the US Embassy on empowering leadership potential and environmental awareness of the youth.

Since 2011, Jen has worked on her own passion of empowering leaders and entrepreneurs to reach their potential to make a difference in the world through teaching soft skills, leading public speaking communities/personal development seminars/training workshops, and writing books in both Asia and Europe. Since then, Jen has started pursue her life career as a performance and leadership trainer, international management consultant, coach, and writer. Till 2018, Jen has published four books "Nonstop living, loving and giving," "The Goal Achiever: the ultimate nine steps to achieve a personal goal (particularly a full scholarship),""Unleash your passion: the ultimate seven pillars toward full potential and fulfilment", The leadership development journey: how entrepreneurs develop their leadership during their lifetime. She is currently working on three other book projects: a 'The YOU journal' book based on a habit-based study; a novel related to women leadership; and a book related to experiences of working with different organisations and actors in society. Jen was awarded as the winner of International Public Speaking Contest in

Malaysia and Vietnam in 2016 and 2018 as well as in the US embassy in 2018. She has been an awarded speaker at different speaking events such as Tedx, Hviet program, Youthspeak, Enterprise conference in Hue University in Vietnam or Collaborative leadership conference in Bradford University in the UK.

Jen is thankful for the different opportunities to continue living, to being loved unconditionally, and to have received all the best things. She has been amazed by every single person she has met who has lived fully, loved completely, and given devotedly. She has been inspired to be nonstop living, loving, and giving every moment of her life and as a duty to inspire people around her to do so.

Meet Jen, join personal development community and get courses, and books and her everyday inspiring stories at the website: jenvuhuong.com/thegoalachiever or email to jenvuhuong@gmail.com

www.ingramcontent.com/pod-product-compliance
Lightning Source LLC
Chambersburg PA
CBHW050456290526
45786CB00006B/2311